Goby Fish and Pistol Shrimp

By Kevin Cunningham

21st Century Junior Library

Published in the United States of America by
Cherry Lake Publishing
Ann Arbor, Michigan
www.cherrylakepublishing.com

Content Adviser: Stephen Ditchkoff, Professor of Wildlife Ecology and Management, Auburn University, Alabama
Reading Adviser: Marla Conn MS, Ed., Literacy specialist, Read-Ability, Inc.

Photo Credits: © Song Heming | Dreamstime.com, cover, 1, 14; © Orlandin | Dreamstime.com - Gold-streaked Prawn-goby And Djeddah Snapping Shrimp Photo, 4; © scubaluna/istock, 6; © Pipehorse | Dreamstime.com - Graysby And Neon Goby Photo, 8; © Stocktrek Images, Inc. / Alamy Stock Photo, 10; © Underwater Imaging / Alamy Stock Photo, 12; © cbimages / Alamy Stock Photo, 16; © Sphinx Wang/Shutterstock, 18; © RGB Ventures / SuperStock / Alamy Stock Photo, 20

Library of Congress Cataloging-in-Publication Data

Names: Cunningham, Kevin, 1966- author.
Title: Goby fish and pistol shrimp / Kevin Cunningham.
Description: Ann Arbor, MI : Cherry Lake Publishing, [2016] | Series: Better together | Audience: K to grade 3. | Includes bibliographical references and index.
Identifiers: LCCN 2015049538| ISBN 9781634710848 (hardcover) | ISBN 9781634712828 (pbk.) | ISBN 9781634711838 (pdf) | ISBN 9781634713818 (ebook)
Subjects: LCSH: Mutualism (Biology)—Juvenile literature. | Gobiidae—Juvenile literature. | Snapping shrimps—Juvenile literature. | Animal behavior—Juvenile literature.
Classification: LCC QL638.G7 C86 2016 | DDC 591.7/85—dc23
LC record available at http://lccn.loc.gov/2015049538

Cherry Lake Publishing would like to acknowledge the work of The Partnership for 21st Century Skills.
Please visit *www.p21.org* for more information.

Printed in the United States of America
Corporate Graphics

CONTENTS

These two animals use teamwork and camouflage to stay safe in the ocean.

Hide and Peek

A small **crustacean** peeks out from a hole in the ocean floor. It cannot see. The **antennae** on its head tell it what is going on. A pistol shrimp must be careful. Many animals in the neighborhood want to eat it.

How does the pistol shrimp stay safe? The goby fish is its **ally**. No one knows why the two animals became partners. But gobies and pistol shrimp work hard to protect each other.

Goby fish are often named after physical traits or other characteristics.

Go Go Gobies

Goby fish live in waters around the world. Scientists have counted more than 2,000 different **species** of gobies.

Some goby species have unusual names. The bumblebee goby is black and yellow like a bee. The longjaw mudsucker crawls in mud.

A goby usually likes to sit on a rock on the seafloor. A suction cup near its rear fins

This small neon goby is getting its meal by cleaning a larger fish.

keeps the fish in place. Few gobies grow larger than 4 inches (10 centimeters) long.

Gobies eat meat. They are **carnivores**. Some goby fish hunt smaller sea creatures. Other goby species get a meal by working as fish cleaners. Large fish allow the neon goby onto its body. The neon goby eats any **parasites** it finds.

Think!

Gobies need tricks to survive. You can see through the crystal goby's body. That's how it got its name. How would being a see-through fish help it avoid hunters?

Pistol shrimp catch their prey in a very unique way.

Big Bang

An adult pistol shrimp is usually between 1 and 2 inches (2.5 and 5 cm) long. One front leg ends in a **pincer**. The other ends in a huge claw called a snapper. The powerful snapper helps the pistol shrimp catch **prey**.

The snap of the huge claw creates a bubble. A split second later, the bubble

How do you think the pistol shrimp got its name?

pops. SNAP! The pop sounds as loud as a gunshot.

The popping bubble sends out a **shock wave**. Prey hit by the shock wave cannot move. The pistol shrimp grabs its hurt prey. It drags the animal home to eat it.

A pistol shrimp lives in a **burrow**, or hole. A burrow is good for hiding. A burrow

Ask Questions!

The pistol shrimp's snapper makes a huge noise. It makes the shrimp one of the ocean's loudest animals. Ask a parent, teacher, or librarian what other sea creatures make loud noises.

These yellow watchman gobies live in the western Pacific Ocean. They share a burrow with a pistol shrimp.

is good for hunting. A burrow makes a great hiding place for gobies, too. The pistol shrimp and goby fish take teamwork to the extreme. They share a home.

Since pistol shrimp cannot see, goby fish are their eyes.

Animal Roommates

Many pistol shrimp species build their burrows in the ocean floor. A few even use their snappers to blast a burrow out of rock.

The pistol shrimp invites a goby fish to share its burrow. Soon the two swim around together. The pistol shrimp puts an antenna on the goby. The goby watches out for **predators**.

Hungry predators search the seafloor for food. But the goby fish and pistol shrimp stay hidden.

What happens when a hungry predator comes near? The goby darts back to the burrow. The pistol shrimp feels it leave. It swims to safety, too. The predator moves past the burrow. It cannot find the goby or the pistol shrimp.

Pistol shrimp **tend** the burrow. Their claws push dirt and sand like a bulldozer. They make the burrow big enough for two.

Look!

One species of pistol shrimp lives in giant groups. Look around the next time you're outside. Do you see any other creature that lives together in a group of hundreds or thousands?

These creatures are safer sticking together than they are on their own.

A burrow can cave in. It might bury the goby. But the fish waits. It knows the pistol shrimp will dig it out.

The pistol shrimp gets a guard. The goby fish gets a safe home. Together, they form one of the most unique animal teams in nature.

GLOSSARY

ally (AL-eye) a creature that helps another creature

antennae (an-TEN-ee) long feelers on the head of a shrimp and other creatures

burrow (BUHR-oh) a hole where an animal lives

carnivores (KAHR-nuh-vorz) creatures that eat only meat

crustacean (kruh-STAY-shuhn) a group of sea animals that includes shrimp and crabs

parasites (PAR-uh-sites) creatures that feed off the body of another creature

pincer (PIN-sur) a claw that can pinch or grab

predators (PRED-uh-turz) animals that hunt other animals for food

prey (PRAY) an animal hunted for food by other animals

shock wave (SHAHK WAYV) a blast that can hurt a creature

species (SPEE-sheez) a certain type of an animal

tend (TEND) take care of

FIND OUT MORE

BOOKS

Jenkins, Steve, with Robin Page. *How to Clean a Hippopotamus: A Look at Unusual Animal Partnerships*. New York: HMH Books, 2010.

Scatina, Michael. *The Goby and the Shrimp*. Oklahoma City: Tate Publishing, 2013.

WEB SITES

Animal Planet: Shrimp and a Goby (video)
www.animalplanet.com/tv-shows/animal-planet-presents/videos/top-10-odd-animal-couples-shrimp-a-goby

Encyclopedia Britannica: Goby
www.britannica.com/animal/goby

National Geographic: Amazing Pistol Shrimp Stun "Gun" (video)
http://video.nationalgeographic.com/video/worlds-deadliest/deadliest-pistol-shrimp

INDEX

ABOUT THE AUTHOR

Kevin Cunningham is the author of more than 60 books. He lives near Chicago.